PANZER HERZ

ALSO BY KYLE DARGAN

The Listening (Cave Canem Prize Winner)

Bouquet of Hungers (Hurston/Wright Legacy Award Winner)

Logorrhea Dementia

Honest Engine (Kingsley Tufts Poetry Award Finalist)

Anagnorisis (Lenore Marshall Prize Winner)

PANZER HERZ
A LIVE DISSECTION ||||| POEMS

KYLE DARGAN

TRIQUARTERLY BOOKS / NORTHWESTERN UNIVERSITY PRESS
EVANSTON, ILLINOIS

TriQuarterly Books
Northwestern University Press
www.nupress.northwestern.edu

Printed in the United States of America

10 9 8 7 6 5 4 3 2 1

ISBN 978-0-8101-4568-9 (paper)
ISBN 978-0-8101-4569-6 (ebook)

Cataloging-in-Publication Data are available from the Library of Congress.

I want to see you game, boys, I want to see you brave and manly,
and I also want to see you gentle and tender.

—THEODORE ROOSEVELT

They only love my armor
and that I'm a performer.

—ANDRÉ 3000

What is it to be "naked" among men, outside of institutional relations, family,
profession, and obligatory camaraderie?

—MICHEL FOUCAULT

To all the killers and the hundred-dollar-billers.
For real niggas who ain't got no feelings.

—PRODIGY

I was a beast, now I'm the jungle.

—DOCTUR DOT

CARDIAC

INCISION
      Pericardiectomy   3

DIASTOLE

Phase I
      King for a Day   9
      Diaspora: A Narcolepsy Hymn   10
      When I Say I Want to Defund the Police   11
      BOOK OF RUTH   14
      Ronin   17
      "What More Could I, a Young Man, Want"   19
      Escapology   20
      Traditional Marriage   22
      Man of the Family II   23
      Mutant Dealing Factor   24
      Performance Studies: Gunslinger   25
      Undertaker   26

Phase II
      Performance Studies: O. P. P.   31
      How I Became a Pleaser   33
      Remedial Heteronormativity   35
      Permutations   37
      Her   38
      Rhythm   39
      Inquiry   41
      Another Me   43

Performance Studies: She Asks "What's Your Fetish"   45
"The Erotic Is a Measure Between"   47

INCISION

Pericardiectomy   51

SYSTOLE
Phase III

For the Man Who Caught My Father   57
I Scream My Throat Raw   59
A Man with Nothing to Lose   60
These Men   62
Chris Christie Waits Alone at Newark Penn Station   64
That Time I Was God   65
Dendrology   66
Since You and I Would Talk about Mars   68
The Venus of Slapboxing   69
After People Stop Asking about Me   70

Phase IV

The Type of Wife I Have Made   73
The Rule of Two   76
Mosaic Mary   78
Minefields   79
Crews   80
Internal Legislation   82
Glass, Once Shattered, Flutters like Paper   83
Love Be a Slow-Moving Storm   85
Another Way to Understand Our Fathers   86
Across Space and Time   87
Small Traveler   88
Adamah / AMAB   89

Suture

Post-Op   93

Acknowledgments   95
Notes   97

INCISION

PERICARDIECTOMY

For how—inside us—it lives, the heart travels modestly. Its pericardium no more ornate than a canvas bladder. A single traveler's suit, which it—the heart—grows to fit snugly over seasons' time. Uniform. It is said of brilliant people: same attire every day. A brilliant motor, the heart. When we say *have a heart*, we maybe mean *be brilliant in your compassion*. What empathetic genius it must take—knowing all the heart knows of us—to still find reasons we might deserve another beat. And another. That enormity—the blood tint rosing our fate's looking glass—all of that clad and strapped within the humble, fibrous pericardium, as if the body, understanding its treasure, instructed the heart *put this on, and hide*.

*　　*　　*

Diagnosis: manhood is just a sack. Or that cis-seeing men relate to it as such. Something to be filled. Something not worth adorning since it comes empty.
　　　　　　　　Plausible: the desire to penetrate others is a vicarious and frightening desire to be *filled*. How tough a never-stretched sack can become. How hard.

At some point, sooner in a self-perceived sack's life than it might imagine, its skin becomes a carapace. That emptiness then, there is no way it may be reached without first cracking the armor that the *sac masculin* has become.

DIASTOLE

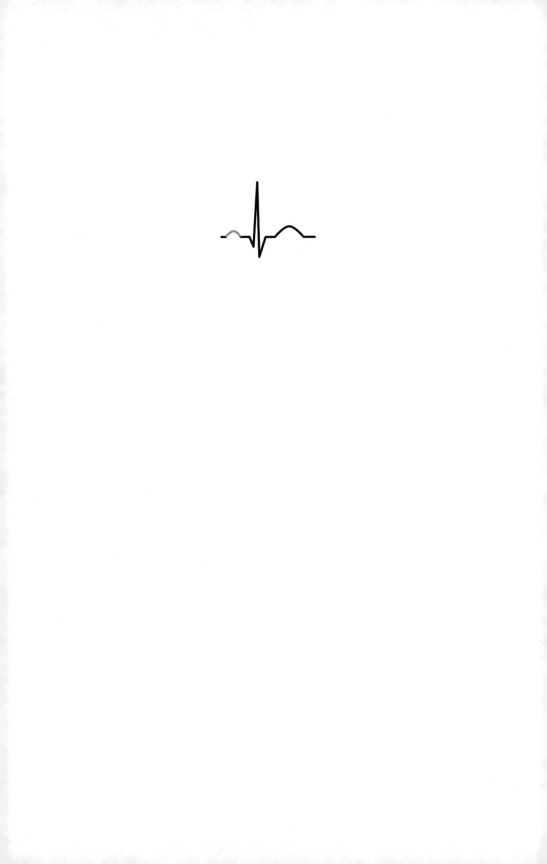

KING FOR A DAY

"Miserable warrior, you are furthest from love."
—THE PRINCE, VINLAND SAGA

Seize a foothill from the ridges peering
            godly from the north. Break it.
Let chisel and sledge   reduce it to torso-
            and skull-sized chunks. Raise the earth
        into a motte. Set your inner castle's stones.
Erect around that keep
                    twelve defensive towers
                    and adjoining curtain walls.
Above the battlements, set on pikes, flown like flags—
the hands   and feet   of your enemies.
And you will require still a proper flag—
                        something to hang
as pennant, emblazoned with the family
            crest you bear. And by *you*
what is embodied is the royal
    we—the serfs and knights and smiths
            who bejewel your crown. And your crown
being nothing more than your one skull,
        and yet a head   you believe so precious
whole geologies had to be re-formed   around it.
O, patchwork   mountain. O, cold abode
of rock. What   little defense will this afford you
when comes tomorrow   the age of cannons.

9

DIASPORA: A NARCOLEPSY HYMN

after Morgan Parker (and Beyoncé and Biggie)

It was all a dream—
seas reigned by a monarchy of islands—rocky scalps claiming *Royal*.
I woke up like this:

July-moist, tumbled in sheets of worn linen sun. Having eloped
with my loneliness, nothing ruled me. Those dowried mangroves?
It was all a dream.

No land. No husbandry. I was the sea—my tides juicy with kelp,
winds fatted by salt. My grandmother's worry was a barque.
I woke up like this,

having slept, my senses ebbed, through her fog bells. I awoke: bright
water. I awoke: a seaway for Moorish vessels. Chattel, colonization,
it was all a dream—

a revisionist slumber, a mirage of moral flawlessness. The Sea of Fog
and Darkness, dark men crossed it first after I carried them to its cusp.
I woke up like this,

those seafarers mused—palms flush with the Americas' new spoils.
I am America's dark soil, not water. Cash crops breaching my back
—it was all a dream,
I woke up—*here*—like this?

WHEN I SAY I WANT TO DEFUND THE POLICE

*There was someone down in the valley because a mountain is not
a mountain if there is nothing below.*
—TA-NEHISI COATES

I mean I have been a boy born breaching
from The Largest City in a small state,

and there, seeking richer breaths, the wind
vanes of my feet would point me southward

towards The Mountain and the little villages
and townships skirting its foothills—where

most of the residents were they who'd fled
from that Largest City with tax base in tow.

And I did not desire migration. I did not want
to shun the gift that what-some-called-riot

and others-called-uprising had given: a colossus
machine of a city. But some days, air was all

I needed. So, again, my sail-feet would whisper
walk south and I would. (I don't know why

some people call police pigs instead of wolves.) I was a boy
watched by wolves—and nothing held against them. The village,

its townsfolk, paid the wolves to be wolves.
And the wolves themselves had boys like me to feed.

Occasionally, we would cross tracks with their boys
on our quests for air—bicycles or basketball courts.

One blacktop afternoon in the village, we gravelly
city boys rubbed rough with the village boys.

Coefficient friction between their shouts and our skin,
and someone called for the wolves and the wolves came

and I watched the wolves arrive inside a larger
wolf with blaring eyes. The wolves opened

the larger wolf's trunk maw, and inside all the teeth—
shotgun upon pistol upon rifle, and we were / were we

just boys. The wolves snarled enough firepower to tuck
a whole village into bloody slumber. If the desire was to daunt

us city boys, to assure *safe* never grazed in our minds
as we moved through the village towards The Mountain,

or anywhere with wolves, then it was a sound investment,
for the memory of that trunk and the wolves armed to the teeth

with teeth never leaves my waking or sleeping mind, ever
breaks the wind at my feet. And what if a terrified boy

does not make the best decisions with his feet
or adrenalin-laced legs? Boys get bitten because

the wolves are paid to bare teeth, paid to bite frightened
things, paid to wolf. And if a city is already making us prey,

I promise you we prey would rather you feed other
mouths than the wolves', that what fungible mana exists

be spread to squirrels that seed the ground, or beavers
that fatten the rivers, or butterflies that pollinate

the trees. All of that grows air, which is what I needed
in The Largest City in the small state. But if you look down

from The Mountain, from the foothill cities, and see pests
of course, your first thought may be, we need more wolves

and more wolves, and more wolves.

BOOK OF RUTH

1.1

A portrait studio's shadow persists inside that skyline—so much as memory's substructure cannot be demolished.

I was *such a happy baby* (something my family has learned to use as euphemism for *what's happened to you*), and Grandma Ruth thought I could make it in New York. A baby model. A little brown joy-bug. She schlepped me from Jersey through the tunnel, up an unending elevator shaft, to a room (four walls still indelible upon the wind despite those towers and many bodies having been razed). I romped with the other tykes while Ruth envisioned magazine spreads, maybe a good check. The time came for me to smile for the camera (I come from a bloodline of performers), but, no—I did not giggle on queue. Though she pleaded, I proved to be the pensive child. The waste of a trip back through traffic to Newark.

Those towers like window dressing since ripped away from that particular pane of daylight. I can see the smudge of us up there. See her wide Broadway grin. See her imploring, all teeth. *Smile, Kyle. Smile.*

*　　*　　*

1.2

There were horses once in Weequahic Park. I cannot fathom their rippling chassis charging around the now paved half-mile oval, but this is true for many things Grandma Ruth told me about old Newark. My deficient imagination. Or my mind trained to see the city as I found it—one National Guard siege worse for wear.

She always spoke of that grandstand. Just east of it, the lake she watched me walk onto one winter as it was iced and snowed over. Falling in was my first physics exam. Her arms pulling me out, my first salvation—the first of many things we'd learn to keep between ourselves.

The lake displaces the racetrack in my memory's legend. Tap that spot: *that's where I almost slipped under.*

Directly north from that point of recall, risen over the tree line, the brown-brick building where she lived. *I can run there*, I told her. Then begged her. Despite the spectre of me watching from under the lake's surface, she lets me trot the mile and half out the park and down Elizabeth Avenue—another thing between her and I. Her thunderbird curbing every few blocks to ask *you OK?* A decade later, I'd be a cross-country athlete, but she hadn't seen the future. What she saw was my will—the same that almost had me drowned in the lake—and she let it run.

*   *   *

1.3

LL says he's *been here for years*. I'm 10 years old—fresh to double dig-
its. I'm ignorant of the backstory for LL's ire. Don't know *Radio*. Don't
know *Deffer*. Then he roars: *What made you forget that I was raw?* Cog-
nitive differentiation is growing within me, though. Neurons stretching
their capacity for metaphor. I watch *Rap City* when Grandma Ruth
gives *Matlock* a rest. There's something choral about the lead sample. The
church in her is compelled to listen with me. We stare at hoodie-veiled
eyes and violent lips. LL clutching the ring announcer's mic. Proclaim-
ing *DAMAGE! DAMAGE! DAMAGE! DAMAGE!* And I don't have
any enemies yet, but I know this is how I want to talk to them once I
do. This incredulous syntax of promised ass-whuppings and destruction.

LL's grandmother cameos at the video's end—after her grandson's flex.
Todd. Todd, get upstairs and take out that garbage. Grandma Ruth and I
debate the import of *trash*. Signifying, I say: the rubbish is the usurper
emcee, the masochistic upstart, to be head-cracked at mama's behest.
Grandma Ruth says it's no marquee opponent. That it's just another
undercard bout of daily work. Poet I'm becoming, of course I think she
doesn't get it. Boy I am, so foolish to doubt her well-labored hands.

*   *   *

RONIN

No lord to my name, no master
to measure my probity with a caressing
stare over my jawline and brow.

New day suns now speak
of walking forward, but to where
must my ambling arrive? I know not
if these roads are truly
dirt beneath me or miraged
overlays upon the earth's entasis—

                            an ocular projection,
                candlelight,
a chorus of dim radiance
beaming from my skull's twin niches.

Let my feet rest. Let me sharpen
my sword—a sliver of mirror
that also severs. I recall
my teachers, the bladework
of their tongues. I am trimmed now,
lean, garnished only with teachings.

But now left only my mind's worn scroll.

I long for one of my teacher's sighs or
warm smirks that sings: *so much in this world*
of which you remain unknowing,
but take my hand and again rise. Always

get up. I long to abandon this violent
vagrancy, but the roads I walk
as a man—terra firmed or imagined—

teem with other men who know
no training, who see upon me
my teachers' marks and ache
for the elicitation of drawn steel.

"WHAT MORE COULD I, A YOUNG MAN, WANT"

Arriving home past my daily   expiration point, I cannot bring
myself to settle my house   into proper repose. I stumble
into slumber leaving bulbs to emanate all night—a burning within
the nest. Set then unattended,   the senile dishwasher churns
into the new day. I awaken   at some odd hour—maybe four.
Shallow sleep bleached by fluorescence. The air tinny with rumpus
of water's steady pelt   against a mixing bowl.
The restlessness of this house   is my own. The wood, the copper,
the brick all remember what they once were: pine tree, palisades,
shale. Lord, how did I   come to preside over this
shrine to repurpose, reduction?   What life do I abandon when
I rise as a working man and toil for this privilege of living alone?

ESCAPOLOGY

I would rather my heart mimic
a David Blaine than a Houdini
—sleights of suffering stillness
for broadcasted lifetimes. Not shocking
audiences by breaking free.

Endurance is not magic,
sadly. Think of everlasting
love as a simple chant—an arcane
language loop that fuses souls
given precise enunciation.
Or am I thinking of sorcery?
(A wizard might wand your lips
into Japanese hornets for calling
him a mere magician.)
                            Regardless,
I admire David Blaine
for the same reasons many
think him a charlatan—that being
he is merely a man, one who'll risk
standing within the icy cage of human
pain until his nerves numb
or he forgets to reclaim consciousness.
My heart—it thinks too much,
sees *opening* as an illusion
disguising constraint. It fidgets,
tucks and rocks with a passion similar
to that with which it first dove
inside romance's straitjacket sleeves.

When freed, my heart clambers
from out the body's river of blood.

Along the banks, the bookies extend
their palms to collect from all the patsies
who bet my heart could
breathe submerged in muddy love.

TRADITIONAL MARRIAGE

I beg your pardon.
I don't care about your rose garden.
I've listened to the things you said.
You just sound like you're scared to death.

I joke with a friend's husband about the anguish of modern commuting. *If only I could swing downtown on a zip-line.* Ha-ha. *Yeah, connect it to poles that changed height. You could zip back home too.* Ha-ha. My Friend, his wife, gives me "the look"—*don't encourage him*. But I'm a poet and he's an engineer—a biologically incorrigible unit. As we must banter, so must she wag her head with chagrin. But by way of parrying the social banality of union till death, we have conceived an all-inertia form of extreme public transportation. I'm already writing the angel investor pitch in my head. He's sketching schematics, while his wife—once my friend, now The Wife—takes brain-notes for the novel that filters her dissatisfaction during these social exchanges. Greatness will sprout from the etiquette of this moment, as it is rude to climb into the marriage box only to later be seen using your clean hands to claw free. Let husbands laugh as "men" laugh. Let "women" sigh as should wives. Smell the smoke—a light focused through the mind's monocle burning a hole in the middle matrimony's playbook. Watch us zip-line through that smoldering portal, lured by something else, anything else, with which we've had yet to grow bored.

Take flight, take flight.
—IDLES

MAN OF THE FAMILY II

Everything sent our father off the top rope—a button lost off our
coats, the carpet bladderbaptized by the cat, or another of Mother's
steady suppers of franks and beans. He became some strange fowl—
Gallo Libre—perched on the banister, arms flapping to amp up
an absent crowd before launching into an airborne pinwheel and
flattening the coffee-table. We went through many coffee-tables—and
mail carriers, and door-to-door evangelists who rang only to be greeted
with a sharp clothesline. The mask—its red sequin comb and wattle—
spared our father retribution when the cops came and found only a
barely refrigerator-tall man holding a can of cheap swill. Eventually,
we saw that it was Mother who would hide his mask beneath the fresh
laundry—nesting it with some compulsory devotion.

MUTANT DEALING FACTOR

My blood cells————produce a potent
    antidepressant————blue humor sought
        for its unique———— compounds   foreign
        to Earth's chemistry———— I activate
      by only thinking————*nothing is unending*
    (which I already————think most hours)
See my arteries————glow & around me
    life decelerates———— Ever walked through
      fire unphased   ————I singe but I do not feel
      If you are honest————you would not covet
    metahumanity   ————My names are *Freak*
Slug   Sociopath———— *Zombie* My cult
of fans bleed———— me (like the thirsty
    needles inside————clandestine genetic labs)
      Some who suffer————imagine I am strong
        Each of my days————is no more than a dead
    lock between my pains————and my "powers"
a stalemate as lethal ————as boredom   I read
in *The Economist*————soon neuroscience will
    target electricity————to hunt depression
      among neurons————In China   a researcher
       deceived two lovers————accessed & CRISPR'd
    their zygote's DNA————when I am right here
they could have asked me————how far I think
we can stretch————the merits of inoculating
    our humanity———— against our human pain
    I with this face————that confesses to no woe
    an anesthetic code————pulsing beneath my skin

PERFORMANCE STUDIES: GUNSLINGER

It's a chancy job, and it makes a man watchful . . .

and a little lonely.

—MATT DILLON

The town is not big enough for the both of them. My father & my father's anxiety about becoming a father. They settle it. Like men. The blood-hungry way. Which means he must get his hands on a gun to be my father, protector of The Expecting and The Expected. A decade forward since the riots, it is Newark dangerous in a different way—the way any hound can get their hind bit when circling too close to the morseled carcass that is the city. But he is having a baby. He has to eat. Has to. Move, and he's going to bury that goddamned anxiety to do so. Tucking the scruffy pistol in his sock. Though that doesn't cure it. I cannot explain how a man loses a gunfight with anxiety, but when it is over, my father has a bullet wound on his foot. While the gun is banished back into the un-serialed shadows. Who knows if the anxiety ever left the city's limits. Might I have seen its own shadow stalking the gray sidewalks in my father's conscious, pointing the same gun my father bought to silence it. Crosshairs glinting in its chatty maw.

UNDERTAKER

I waste away for fun
I am my father's son
His shadow weighs a tonne
—IDLES

The rich man and the poor—
they taste alike to the grave,
and I have my own boys to feed.

So I am obliged to upsell:
a gilded casket
to carry the late Senator.
                    I am
an expert in disposable
income—what some will pay

for frills they will never
remember feeling, death's
delicacies.
                    Even if
rebirth is not a lie,
no newborn arrives

crying over the satin
that did not line
a prior life's final bed.

I've made it known
I'm only to be buried
in sand. May it polish

my skeleton slowly.
May I gleam for the day
our planet trembles apart

and our interred bones break
free—alphabets set adrift
among the punctuation of stars.

PERFORMANCE STUDIES:
O. P. P.

It was Magic that summer, when our tracks wound
long between the loci of Crescent Road and Prospect
Street. On foot, we carried our noise
from one to the other. The sub-ground
walls of apartment buildings' garages
kept us from cutting through backyards,
kept us moving in knights' Ls—intersection
to intersection, long avenues made for rooks
or teenagers whose urban costumes fit them
ill as legacies.
                 Climbing to the top floor
in one of Prospect's proud brick buildings,
Mrs. Roach and my grandmother were already cooking
scandal. Speculation stewed between them
and I watched their lips pause for re-aired news.
California | Earvin Johnson | HIV. Around me,
the ladies spat "tsk" and guessed at Cookie's fate.

Down Park Ave., over Glenwood to Jason's driveway court.
A game of 21—running hookshots tolled the backboard
where all we asked was "You heard?" We knew
little of what made "the hiv" but swore
by thin knowledge of how to prevent it.
In Jason's bedroom studio we freestyled goofy
lyrics, deepened our voices to discern.
"Should've used a prophylactic" I barked
like a Cypress Hill chorus or a Kane
crescendo: *put a quarter in your ass*
'cause you played yourself. I'd choke on shame,
three years later, when a health teacher corrected me
on the role mouths could play in transmission.

Terror, then, was learning I was one wrong answer
away from being like Magic. Maybe one
pair of lips—another's, my own. I wanted
to go back and rescind those lips that made rhymes
as a child. We'd just sealed the '80s, remember?
Reagan's vacant smile haunted our homes, hip-hop
was too busy for compassion, while we were fly
as we weaved music of other people's pain.

HOW I BECAME A PLEASER

It is the first time that my mouth twists
death's doorknob. Aboard *The Horizon*,
an economy cruise ship routed down
the murky Gulf Coast, I am twelve,
maybe—I can't accept that my mother
loves my stepfather so deeply
that she'll belt into a tabletop P.A.
system that *he* would be her choice
companion if she ever found herself
deserted on an island. I'm in the pool—
arms and legs blunt scissors chopping
the chlorine-sharp water. Liquid's
ability to lift—I wade at the edge,
contemplating what it means to float
upon something itself floating. I notice
a voice. I gaze up and find my new friend—
a girl. A new girl. Not a girl I know from school.
A new frontier. She whispers. Water
lodged in my ear. "Will you *go* with me?"
I've yet for a girl to ask me such a thing,
but I know it's not a navigational query.
"Nope," I reply flatly, and in an instant,
her feet find my shoulders, shoving me
beneath the sloshing surface. She can't see
I'm smiling. It's all fun until her heels
begin to pummel my skull's crown.
Concussed and sinking towards
an unlikely demise at sea, my mind
throbs with one goal—*get clear of her legs*.
My lungs taste implosion. Adrenal glands
commandeer my limbs and conduct fury.
I somehow emerge to suck salt-crisp air.
Lost in piña coladas and new love, my mother
has no idea I almost drowned. I survive

this initial lesson in the dangers of daring
to defy what another's heart has decreed.
I hack and wheeze my way from out the pool,
memorizing this secret: the stern cheeks and
gorgon braids of the girl who almost sunk me.

REMEDIAL HETERONORMATIVITY

"Man-law" I first violate at age ten—
my wandering fingers not appeased by picking
through my cousin's video
game cartridges, *Sports Illustrated*s.
Rather, I let my tips trace their way
around his bedroom—exhuming
sheathed *New Mutants* and *Excalibur*s,
probing for more between the expansive cleavage
of seat cushions.

It is true—if you are committed
to finding something, you will
discover something. I wondered how
it would feel for me to be, like him,
male and free from adolescence.
When my fingers grazed a waxy *Playboy*
wedged between sofa frame and metal
fold-out, I did not peel open the cover.
The need to testify kept me from yielding
command over my eyes and hands to center-
folds of ballyhooed skin—alabaster,
unattainable. In the moment, a budding
knowledge: my cousin's lust
and where he hid it. I stowed
both under my tongue—the weight

an ache within my jaw. I found Uncle
downstairs at the old walnut table,
air thick with aromas of crossword
ink and Parliament smoke. After I tattled
about his son's hoarded fantasy,
Uncle's disdain pulled up a chair, sat
cloaked in authority's masking musk.
"So what? At least the boy isn't gay."

The burning floor of my mouth
awash in his lesson: his new naming
of deviance. And how intolerable this
name compared to whatever ogling
my cousin did in secret, fancying
himself grown. And how not to take the hint
that if I synced my sight with the spreads'
flaying gaze, I too could be dispatched
into what proper yearning awaited beyond
the proving ground of my boyhood?

Once there, I could be like my cousin—maybe
sullied, still redeemed—but only after
I learned to narrow my eyes, to mouth
Father spare the boys who, kilned
in the same heat as me, risked hiding
other men's skin beneath their beds.

PERMUTATIONS

Women want him. Men want to be him.
Some men want him. Some women long
for one another, not a him. Other "women"
know themselves to be "men," while other
"men" "women." He wants

                                 that which they all want
—to be plainly wanted, to be a hook
needle threaded by another's want,   knot-kissed
at the eye, plunging through and drawing
the breached fabrics of *who* and *I am*.
Flimsy throughout life, men and women
unraveling. So many want that fraying
to take them faster, gender's textile
de-helixing back to unspooled thread.

HER

I remember the initial ascent
up their porch stairs, her older sister
opening the double-doors—sistergirl
stare as though I was some sorrow
salesman come knocking. I remember
waiting in their parlor, her father
sternly ignoring me. I remember
the staircase creaking as she descended,
gorgeous in a way that only
another fourteen-year-old can find
a fourteen-year-old gorgeous. My sweet
breath brûléed, stomach in plummet,
I remember feeling hollow.
There are parts I've chosen to forget.
I recall her asking if I'd escort her around
the block's tight orbit. Her little
brother had to come. I carried him
on my shoulders. We were a play
family, that's how I remember it felt.
She was my first fall. We were joined
in my head. What other wanting
could puberty need to show me,
teach me? I remember believing
I had crossed some threshold,
but it would be a slow march of years
before she would ever kiss me—tipsy
twenty-somethings on a late drive home.
She queried, "Can I ask you something
and you can't say *no*?" I cannot
remember my response as she climbed
over the gear shift, obscuring the already
dark road. We almost crashed.
I remember it as flying.

RHYTHM

With a fuel tank full of testosterone,
the procreative drive wedged
like a brick against my throttle,
I break to bail from atop my lover
at orgasm's cusp—my basting seed
a road winding away from her abdomen.
I don't feel guilt, but I say *sorry*
for the wreck of me on her skin.
This maneuver a choice of many men
who want to feel but not to father.

While terror's chill is fresh in me—my body
trembling above my own source-code
pooled in her belly button—I question
how is it that I've arrived here again,
taunting new life. It begins with her
profession: *I trust you.* I am aware
that I can't be trusted to police nature
so that not I but my gametes arrive lost
and panicked—so near their rallying
point, so certain to perish with mission
failed.

This dismount some men consider
not contraception but, rather, a parry—
one we might not need were we more
honest about our need to shame women
who do not want to mother but want
to feel. Not trusted with choice or birth
control, she is left to trust my hips'
reflexes in the name of pleasure,
that human pursuit. Her faith as much
a surrender to this world of outcomes
curated, controlled, from the daises of men.

She has to hope that my desire to blend
our bodies but not beget will protect us
both. Though if I pull back a moment
too late, only she will be altered, be *with*.

And to remain is another decision she must
entrust me with, as she would carry. So many
like her must rest faith in men like me—
men whose hearts might fill with helium,
who could peer below and find nothing
tethers them to the duets they leave
within uteri, who can't even be expected
to sing a *sorry* as music begins to swell within.

INQUIRY

"People ask penis questions all the time. Other men want to
know what other men are built like, because that's your biggest
insecurity. You have two insecurities—your money and your dick.
Those are your two insecurities, and if you don't have enough of
either, you feel inadequate."
—KARRINE STEFFANS

The lover who said—as a mid-coitus
ovation—*I wish I could loan you
to my friends*, she is the same woman,
the only woman, who made me
cry with a plain-worded quip. The welling
tears pried open my battened eyelids
after she asked why I did not dress
sharper. I can still only guess at which
I resented more in that moment of rush
hour clamor on the Metro Center
platform—her words or my wounding?

I was twenty-six, grad-schooling
off $10,000 and the small checks
my grandmother mailed me. That was
the answer I did not unwrap and offer her.
Instead, I swallowed. Instead, I vowed
from then on that every orgasm I roiled
from her body would be a vengeance. See,
you think about *visciousness* meaning
you think about how it would
never become you, no? But you are
only deluding until you've realized
you have power and choose not restraint
but to wield it over another, over one
who has hurt you. (*What do you have to say
when my flesh makes you forget my outfits?*)

I have never inquired about the size
and shape of prior men, but after her
each time I entered a lover, I entered
with the intent of leaving pleasure's
floodmark—an out-of-reach notch
placed for nostalgia to lacquer, left to sting
the longer it went unprobed by another.

That woman left me
feeling lost within my own garments.
A poor man, it is said, *is like a foreigner
in his own country.* I learned
how to stitch my flag, how to empire others'
ecstasy. Yes, my skin is a revisionist
history that favors its scars
but, over it, I wear fine clothes now.

ANOTHER ME

My transcript attests to it, so let it be
true: third year, I registered for PSYC 101,
having failed to distinguish *psychology*
from *psychiatry*. Nevertheless,
there were requirements to be fulfilled.
Shakespeare and Chaucer were granted
enough annexing of my gray matter.
Wouldn't psychology teach me how
one redeems his mind's territories?
There was, too, an incentive—the friend
who suggested we both enroll, the friend
I called a sister as a way of staving off
any attraction. Practically a rite of passage—
the course one takes because the eyes,
as much as the brain, need to be fed.
And how I discredited my eyes
after their tracing of her skin lead me
into a semester-worth of notes
on dopamine, endorphins, GABA—
all alienesque neurons, no psycho
-analysis. The midterm's jargon glut
frenzied us into library sessions and
study dates at my upper-class dorm.
We drilled neurotransmitters,
labeled cell parts until our eyelids failed
under the weight of dendrites and synapses.
One night, she asked if she might crash
on our couch—what play-siblings do
—but when she woke, she thanked me
for not touching her while she purred,
prone there. (*Mental confusion:
a state characterized by a lack of clear
and orderly thought.*) That me, suddenly,
did not know who he was. Could he

be brother to someone who could
suspect him a rapist? (*Anticipation:*
the imagining of a future event, which elicits
an emotional response.) That night, that me
convinced himself that his character
was the victim. That me
groaned that men might as well act
as they are typecast.
That me disowned that sister
who was not a sister but a young woman
he found comely. When another me,
years later, revisits that night, he does so
understanding how little it takes for women's
bodies to become bounty in men's minds.
Cognitive dissonance makes it possible
to rationalize rape—another concept
we would not study that semester.
What I learned: that trust can mute stress
so one may slumber. What I learned:
that for prey, experience is a spectrum
blurring the safe wavelengths of light.
What I have learned: that when men yowl
there's no understanding women, many of us mean
we've sat for the test without studying
and resent the possibility of being wrong.

PERFORMANCE STUDIES:
SHE ASKS "WHAT'S YOUR FETISH"

And to be fair to her, I tacked us in that direction.
Her with vid after vid, all breasts all the time—like ESPN
but with breasts. Or maybe just like ESPN (how spectator
sports tossed cheerleaders about for fear of men
getting too aroused around their mere selves).
I want to tell her that I am miffed, honestly—
that my titillation is not a one-chord song,
that she is assuming I am just some nipple trap
in wait to spring, some Neanderthal. (Not fair
to Neanderthals—I know nothing of their kink.)
But I do not type that. Instead I key "clearly
someone has a breast fetish, lol." I am flirty.
(I am passive aggressive.) "But I ain't mad.
I appreciate it." And she does not respond.
Instead she asks "what's your fetish?" More
and more, I question if our lives are mere engagement
with A.I. programmed to feed our human self-
importance? It is a useful skepticism to cultivate
in these times. Maybe she is not that contriving.
She could plainly want to know, want to offer
what she cannot unless I reveal, unless I own
my desire. I type   "I don't know," type
"that's a good question." Which is true, as no answer
rushes from my cerebral sac or my scrotum. I rummage
within the pocket of myself—looking for that key
or quarter, that fetish I could have sworn
I put in there, somewhere. But nothing. And empty-
handed, I type on—as not to hint I might not know
myself enough to answer the simple question.
"Can I have a you fetish? Is that a thing?"
(The itch I don't own is that she reminds me
of someone loved and gone—her face, her bearing
shoulders, ballasted ass? My god, the dizzying

jolt of being snatched out of what you wanted
to believe was intimacy.) "Lmaooo"
she types. "Well I like that," but I have closed
the app—remaining to her, to myself, unrecognized.

"THE EROTIC IS A MEASURE BETWEEN"

after Lorde

Your body is not my pommel horse
nor my Olympic pool or diving board.
Your body is not my personal internet
channel nor my timeline,
nor my warm Apollo spotlight.
Your body is not my award
gala. Your body is not my game—
preseason or playoffs.
Your body is not my political party
convention. Your body is not
my frontline or my war's theater.
Your body is not my time
trial. Your body is not my entrance
exam or naturalization interview.
I am a citizen of this skin—that
alone—and yours is not to be
passed nor won. What is done—
when we let our bodies sharpen
the graphite of each other's bodies
—is not my test, not my solo
show. One day I'll learn. I'll prove
I know how to lay with you without
anticipating the scorecards of your eyes,
how I might merely abide—we two
unseated, equidistant from the wings
in a beating black box, all stage.

INCISION

PERICARDIECTOMY

The gift that is the heart asphyxiates easily.
Wrapped about the heart.   To wrap the mind
about pericarditis,   think first of inflammation,
how it fries our flesh   of its give.
To wrap the heart,   you need two layers—
      one to hug   close the beating
      one to graze the sternum.   Between those two,
      a gracious   glaze of fluid.
But let that glaze of fluid   become a swell.
But let that two-ply   membrane burn with blood.
The pericardium becomes a corset of calcified or billowing tissue.
The heart then a body held captive in haute pain.
The heart was not meant to suffer for fashion.
After a pose on the X-ray's runway, it must be freed of the look.
They take a needle and release ribbons red and wet.
They take a cautery, feather open the leathered flesh, and pull and pleat
and pull and pleat for life.

*   *   *

Forgive me. Brother, you are not empty. Brother.
                        You are airy. You
expand, or long to.   Involuntarily   like a heart, you are
in swell Brother. You could power a moon
      colony with the energy you use to resist the expansive impulse.
The way holding a breath hurts. You're that sentient searing.
      Brother, you
conflate the hurt we never chose, being alive,
with the hurt we, being human, have learned to assign ourselves.

Many of us did not have a choice, Brother, to be Brother or to be Brother how
      we might imagine it.   And it is imaginary, even the Brotherhood
         you believe in   and have been killing for,
                      for yourself and others.
         (You profess to love both.)

Forgive me. Can we break. Or maybe break bread? I am thinking
biscuits—the quick kind. You are
silently starved, are you not? I have the stove
preheating. I've been rumbling through the bakeware.
You take the spoon, though. You peel off the labeling. You press the curved
metal along the seams of the packing.   Until it bursts (I know you love
that part) and the dough releases into forms that the can could never imagine.

There is no meal for us until that.

SYSTOLE

FOR THE MAN WHO CAUGHT MY FATHER

when he lilted—lost in fainting—and careened off the barstool.

Dear Catcher, Dear Hands, I pray you
know this is not just another tale about a dad

and liquor. You know something about my father even I do not:

his weight in plummet, and the necessary
force to keep his shoulders from plowing

into the floor or his temple from tasting the chrome

legs of the stool beside him. As it stands,
this is a tale of a man with bones

well-trod by tobacco and hard spirits. I have been

a character in this story you have
now saved. Yes, I am the one

who crawled free from ash swells, who has never

been whiskey-drowned, who would leave home
to alight from trains in towns where none knew

his damp, cigarette-singed skin. Kissing the phone

screen against my cheek, I try to deduce the cause
of father's fall. A doctor, one month prior,

(what I know which you did not) snaked a balloon through

my father's arteries so hard they collapsed—
a stent left as scaffolding in the unstable

blood shaft. I fathom he maybe lowered himself

        awkwardly upon the seat, with his thigh
    spilling over the edge, the mesh holding

his peripheral artery open to blood instead

        pinched narrow—what the doctor feared
    when he ordered *no more racquetball.*

Couldn't that drive a man to seek a pity drink, to grab

        a seat at the bar—ergonomics
    be dammed and his blood pressure sinking?

You held my father until the ambulance carried him

        to the hospital that let him go,
    tests cleared. And I can only ponder

any of that. I can only write this now at a distance,

        at ease, because you, Dear Arms, snapped
    open—that human preservation reflex—

and embraced his payload which, had it crashed,

would have made
a crypt of me.

I SCREAM MY THROAT RAW

into the sky   between the new high-rises
        plumb like glass   tombstones above The City I Knew
into the guest room   whose only guest has become my screaming
into the washing machine's drum
into the mirror   into the eyes of the fool   there always wearing
    the same stains
into the particulate-rich air I want to tremble
    with someone else's voice   not mine
into a temporary existence where I am all-throat   something
        akin to a star   a fury of hydrogen and helium   that will be
            heard far after I have extinguished
into the theoretical box of time   there is no echo
        as the walls have not proved finished
into my own head   (fist over my mouth)   there is always an echo
        a congregation of all the screams I don't scream at youyouyouyouyou
            but I should   it has to be healthier than this
                my own rage going viral inside me

A MAN WITH NOTHING TO LOSE

But my loyalty
    points—my purchasing
    power. Nothing.

But my economies
    of scale, my digital
    compression :: companionship.

But my all-
    you-can-eat
    loneliness, my rail-
    rapid integration.

But my market-
    driven love
    handles, my accrued
    vacancy.

But my taste
    in artisanal
    bootstrapism.

But my choice
    of protein, of pit-baked
    avarice, of indulgences.
    [CHURCH collects
    as does CAESAR.]

But my supply-
    side floods, my oh
    so buoyant home
    staked and sandbagged
    on striving's pebbly shore.

But my internal
    combustion, my miles,
    my carcinogenic
    Kingdom Come. Nothing.

But my fast casual
    history—every morsel
    wrapped in a bank-
    note's blood-sketched
    hagiography.

But my user-friendly
    righteousness, my Gross
    Domestic Amnesia.
    [*In place of the old wants . . .*
    we finds new wants.]

But my comfort,
    my tariffed aches,
    my engorged
    prerogatives. [*I made*
    this money,
    you didn't. Right, Ted?]

But my ability to believe
    that what I've paid for,
    I have made. Nothing
    to lose, except ownership
    of this wallet-sized tomb—
    these six crisp walls.

But my chains—

THESE MEN

The Painter   speaks to me about the walls—crisp, famished
barriers. *The new gypsum is thirsty. If you don't prime,
it will drink the paint.*
I have been warned: a house is like a child. Always
hungry. Always a new need nibbling into your coffers.

The Glazier   warns me first: *Don't get married*—his finishing
touch upon replacing the inner pane of a tilt-in
basement window. *A wife will bleed you.*
Like a house?   I ponder, but, no. The house is an asset, is an
opportunity
for the men to fix small things I'll learn to google and fix myself
in years' time.
None of the contractors suggest a house is like a wife.

The Electrician cuts me a deal for helping him snake
new wire up the wall cavities. *No good* slips
free from the garrote of smoke in his throat
as he thumbs the worn paper casing off old wire.
A fire hazard. Deadly.
Like a house. Or like a wife, according to

The Plumber   who seems to not want to go home. *Come,
let me show you how to replace a flapper
so you won't have to call me again. I'm expensive.*
The house will bleed me regardless, no? No matter how much
the men show me about how I am to attend to its repair? (Yes.
The answer is yes. It breaks like a marriage—in the places
you've taken your eyes off. It will cost you.)

The Inspector   told me it was a solid home. The contractors pry
                veneer off his name. *Those assholes. Just hungry for closings
                and kickbacks. Always get your own inspector,*
        as if I'll ever buy another house. And I go on to meet
        women who tell me I'll need to sell my house. That we'd need
        a fresh start if we ever married. That my house was too much
        mine. And then I knew too I would never get married.

The Locksmith   said nothing about houses, nor wives. He was the first
                I called back when the house was so bare
                it frightened me. (I've heard an unhoused
                man say you search for a safe place, not a comfortable one,
                and then you put down your head.) The locksmith
                rekeyed the doors (a shamefully DIY task I learn),
                and as he clanked away, I asked if he had one of those
                eye holes. *A door viewer! Yes, I can do that.* With a drill bit
                shaped like a pike, he bored the door's thick grain,
                then squeaked the entry oculus into place. *Take a look.*
                The convex vista seemed distorted, but I could see
                the world—that place so many of these men resent
                having to take refuge from inside houses.

CHRIS CHRISTIE WAITS ALONE
AT NEWARK PENN STATION

Can never trust a fat man. Can't control his impulses
or appetite—what uncle would say when, over dinner
chatterings, the then governor's name arose. Today,
his walk is a lumber—a weight informed by more than flesh
stores clad in untailored blues, a pink tie. He finds a way
to blend into the peeling pillar-scape of the platform's
far-south end. I left the Garden State long ago. My mouth doesn't
ferment the disdain of my uncle and father, their state pensions—
fucking Christie, that asshole. The D.C.-bound Amtrak hisses
and rings its way onto track three, and the ex-governor stands
mostly unmolested except for one transit cop who trots over
to shake hands with an earnestness so rich it could fondant a brick.
What else would be worth his risk of standing in public—to savor
the sweet zealotry of the few who will never not love you?

THAT TIME I WAS GOD

And, demurred, my partner beseeched that I answer if it was alright if she masturbated. When we were apart. She was not seeking blessing but confirmed righteousness. I was unprepared for the question. Understandably. As no one had warned me I was God. And though, of course, I knew the answer (for I was God), I had none of the necessary practice at balancing my incredulity at her need to even ask and my pity at her ever feeling that need. You burn a lot of calories presiding over another's imagination. I was in such good shape then. Instead of prayers I got requests for sexts. Which I fulfilled like a lazy god. What I could have demanded in exchange had I been more strategic. But I was new to the trade. All the other gods I knew, how their women suffered. How quick they were to text me the proof of their women's devotion, which in part is why I never wanted to be a god in the first place. Absolute power corrupts absolutely. My mother had taught me that. Though she was speaking of the gods that lived in City Hall. Who had run our city for years. Who she too served. Maybe mother always saw the god in me. Maybe it explains how we are more *care* than *close*. Gods and devotees do not speak. A same language. Maybe that is what spoiled my ear. That time was God. And for the first time, I could hear so painfully. So clear—what this rule was asking of me.

DENDROLOGY

Kneeling before the Trouble Tree,
the father lofts his voice into the branches
until tribulation drains from his diaphragm.
  As he's done since a young man,
he shuts his eyes, stretches his rib cage
and gropes among the leaves for fruit—

foretasting his teeth snapping through
waxy skin. He knows, when the flesh
beneath is sweet, that his trouble is ripe
and will change no more. Bitterness
on the tongue implies the fibers foresee
room yet for a trouble to mature.

The man has never led his children down
into the grove so they might genuflect
like their father before the Trouble Tree.
They've grown up in this new century, new
country, grown of this soil in which he planted
the burlap-bundled roots from a faraway home.

He's instead let his offspring cure
in the new world's sweet profusion—
all of childhood suffering's wet heft
drawn out from their lungs. What could they
ever breathe into the tree? Could their palates bear
life's casual acerbity? His concern keeps him
coming before the bark—plucking
sour knot after sour knot,
spitting the seeds at his vagrant feet.

On the walk home from the grove—
dirt giving way to a paved walk
—he is met by his youngest girl,

all tears and hands pinpricked
from reaching into the brambles
for the blackberries she'd grown
accustomed to plucking from a bowl.
He kisses the blood from her fingers
and leads her back through the dusk.

And this night, he sleeps easier—
his window open to hear her
whimpers and the tree's pained leaves
rustling, resisting the winds.

SINCE YOU AND I WOULD TALK ABOUT MARS

—for Joeanna

Suppose your love was that fourth planet from the Sun.
I would suit up for the guarantee
                                of nothing more than a mission
              launch on a shuttle
none at NASA were sure held enough fuel celled for the there-
                                        and-back. Just to maybe touch-
down on your rusted soil. I'd take the trip
if only for the small hope. I'd take the trip
for the mere chance of seeing your love closer
than I can see it from here and now—lucky enough maybe
to get to feel the gravity of you,   which balloons the blood-
sponge marrow within me. Read my manifest:
I do not carry as cargo any to seed
my flag there, to reface then populate myself
all over the planet that is your love. As it is   that is the only way
I want it explored—be it escaping
radiation in a dry cove   or letting   the flailing
dust map lines on my gloved hands.
This earth currently beneath my toes
is doomed to crumble. And even with my vigor,
mortality would call to me long before any astral apocalypse—
which is to say, do not see my interplanetary longing
to travel to your love as an escape, as a desperate leap
for survival. *I'll live a lush life* here. But.
To be Mars-bound—that pull is too strong to honestly expect
                my feet could be satisfied on Earth
where, even with my eyes closed, my irises'
                atmosphere remains pierced by your red.

THE VENUS OF SLAPBOXING

My sister pronounced her disapproval
with a certain contrapposto—her neck
cricked to the side, chin tucked to collar-
bone as if to say "Oh, *really?*"
Then followed the soft-sculpting
of her frame. From first rib through
right leg, she cured like a brick arch.
Her arms raised into brimming Vs
set for mantis snaps. Suddenly,
your name was "punk" or "heifer"—
either an ominous thing.

I danced around all her invitations to spar.
Not once did I witness her storied bouts.
I wondered if she even needed to fight.
Did her mere stance forecast a cyclone
of knuckles none wished to dance within?

It did that, the city—turned girls
into forces of nature. Furious, short-lived.

On Alabama Ave, as I watch a man
slapbox with a woman under the V8 bus
shelter, my feet understand the measured
distance he keeps between himself
and her form. It's the same space I held
between myself and my sister—the distance
any wise fool knows to maintain
between himself and a decided woman,
between his chin and her yet to be thrown blows.

AFTER PEOPLE STOP ASKING ABOUT ME

—circa 2019

But everyone asks how is it to raise a daughter within
                this hissy fit christened *Trump's America*. My daughter's
breach into life: five months after that vote, that incision.
                She's two now, can count her own
way to sixteen. Knows maybe thirty animals. Orange
                or any other color remains uncoded
in her mind. She does not see any of *this*. Her world
                is chirping "bye-bye" to the bubbles in her bath
before she sleeps. Yes, it is harder than you might think
                to teach a being concepts you cannot recall
learning yourself. Repetition is useful, as is multisensory
                reinforcement. So raising my daughter in this moment,
that is what it feels like—finding so many ways to repeat
                one concept until it implants and she commands
a new pathway for communing with the world. It is work
                but it does not break me. In fact, I feel spared
the sullied now until we were engaged in something innocent
                like a ride on the kiddie train through Wheaton
Regional Park. Not rearing, just cradling her legs in my lap—
                those instances   when I regain my selfish
mind, its capacity to ponder how many years it might take
                to make this the America in which my kiddo can count
on having fewer rights than her grandmother enjoyed,
                or her great-grandmother who lived a life of dodging
dangerous men—even after she'd joined the police, kept a sidearm.
                But who wants that escaping my mouth?
I instead just point towards trees flanking the tiny tracks,
                beckoning, "*Hoo's* that? Yes, baby. It is an owl."

THE TYPE OF WIFE I HAVE MADE

I have already made a home. The sketch-
pad of my thirties spent practicing

and tracing all I had learned listening
to the lilts of my mother's disappointment

with my father, my stepfather. I am
inclined to think I am the type of Wife

my mother could have really loved.
I chef. I dispatch laundry and dishes.

I start the renovations. I finish them
too. I come home. I always come home.

When I attract those like my mother—women
worked and worked over to the point of wanting

to not be a Wife—no worry then,
as I tend to have the wifing covered.

I own the house, legally but psychically too.
I dominate the house. But I will submit

against a woman's needs, her stress silence,
her arm's length. I am a good subject,

in the colonial sense. I am a Wife. Flag me.
Help yourself to my domestic production.

What good could it do me, a good Wife,
alone? My thirties—a soundproofed house

of prayer, where I never prayed
given my unflagging belief that I was a Wife,

that of the many women unfed by the defunct
ways of wifedom, one of them would love

to recline, de-heel and allow I do the cooking.
I felt secure, and at peace with, the aproned

comfort of posing in that second slot
on the fuck | marry | kill chart. And yet I am

two years past forty and never has a pairing
granted me more than one birthday or New Year's

or Valentine's. Enough sex, certainly. Plenty
women who looped through the cul de sac

of my queen bed. But wasn't I to be a Wife? I am
unpaired—some free radical's looping particle. I have been,

to fistfuls of women, that first slot—never dying
but called again and again to be fucked (though I provided

most of the fucking). I convinced myself
I was destined to be the married, the one

peering down from atop the mound of years
at the skewered carcasses of the killed men

and the stiff bodies of the men whose crotches
glistened only from within the amber of nostalgia.

I would have done well as a modern woman's Wife.
Instead I spend the mending hours pondering why

so many women took me
but never took me in. Me: a *homebody*—a fantasy

for those inclined to see themselves as no more than
visitors, shoal as my mother and I remain. To this day.

THE RULE OF TWO

Lo, the sweet idiocy sung by those who love me: *you are the type of man*
                                            who should have a lot of children.
No thought of finding or proving the existence of the woman who would
tolerate that existence with me,   *for* me.   And, too,
I know they are not envisioning a steadied happiness for my life.
                            They have seen me Involved™.   They have
seen me as breeder—clearly [the CV that is the flesh of my flesh].
The forces
of dad-starved children   and child-started mothers,
            they foresee me settling discord to equilibrium.

I also call this the Blk Dad at the Playground Effect—when suddenly
                                            you become the beacon
   for eight or more free-range kids who have tuned to the orientation
between you and your child, mothers who have released their children
to be released off monkey bars into your unknown arms.   People trust me
too quickly with their children. I do not see myself enough to know
what they see. What they clearly do not know is that I am studying
                        the ways of the Sith. That I have become a firm
believer in The Rule of Two—a master, an apprentice, and no more.
I am only interested in training this one, born of my own force.   Only one
rival to my seat,   via the path of exclusive tutelage—such as the distinction
                        between anger and spite, and how to refine
one into the more focused other. Which is which, you ask, but why
would I show you? You do not possess more potential than my child.
      You do not tempt me
                                    to groom another apprentice.
I have my one. We have our dyad of a galaxy, in which I am aether and
      she is sun.
In which she will expand to combust me   but so is the way of the Sith,

So is the blood-arc that builds towards lordship's apex.

Now why would I desire to tend to a flock
                when I could rear one supreme   predator?

MOSAIC MARY

Scars like lips sewn shut
—humming choirs—cover
the meaty resting arms
of the woman seated near me.
This mother, I have seen her
before shouldering one baby
while lugging two toddlers.
In that way, I know her
to be *blessed*, and then I don't
want to understand her body
as an object of assault,
but she bears the marks
many neighborhood girls
share—lesions more common
than rare around here.
More common to be called
babymama or *bitch* when
the mouths of block boys
open, when their fists close.
Say motherhood is a knife
fight with time. Say that
womanhood is a battle
against having your claws
clipped. Either will leave skin
covered with darkened wound
-mouths—unwavering, subliminal
testimony that what claims
woman does not need sanctimony
for it can and will defend itself.

MINEFIELDS

Remember that men don't behave as they do in the movies—you won't hear a *click* or generally catch any caution before the man is activated. Men may be encased in cloth, plastic, or their mere tufted hide, so a metal detector won't necessarily alert you. Be mindful of withholding speech when you are in a manned area. The frequencies of your silence may cause certain types of men to detonate. If other men are present, the detonation of one man may set off a chain reaction. Areas experiencing armed conflict are clearly high-risk, but men remain dangerous long after the cessation of hostilities. Though you can't count on manned areas being marked, heed warning signs—often, but not always, red. And they rarely say "MEN" or "DANGER." Where signs aren't present, improvised warnings are often used, such as blood-crusted smiles (indicating a crossed boundary), untouched SAFE kits, torn blouses quilted into flags, hair tied to trees. Never assume a recently "cleared" area is safe. Man removal is a difficult and tricky process. It's not unusual for men to remain in an area that has officially been cleared. One reason for this is that men buried in the ground for a long time may sink substantially. Men can't be buried in roads paved for dialogue. Keep in mind, however, that men may be wedged in potholes, or tripwires tied to men on the periphery may be drawn across those roads. Should you suspect that you have entered a manned area—either because you see warning signs, you see a man or potential man, or because a detonation occurs—keep your wits and carefully retreat from danger by backing into your own footsteps. If you can't see your footprints to backtrack, move forward little by little. You'll need to probe the ground for men—probe the ground very carefully. Use your hands or feet. Use your pen or knife. Probe at an angle rather than straight down, since men are easily detonated by top-down pressure. Be wary of picking up anything. Many men are booby traps. You think you're picking up a song, a shield, or a heart, then, lo and behold, there's a man inside. Even god-vows and children are used as bait. Rule one of keeping your thumbs: if you didn't drop it, don't pick it up. If you find yourself the leader in a situation, you'll have to coach every member of your troupe on how to exit a manned area safely. Make sure you're all talking, that you're on the same page, because one wrong move could get everyone killed.

CREWS

Those Clay Terrace
boys. Those
Benning Park boys.
Those Simple
City boys.
Those River Terrace
boys. After hours
those boys. Those
pop-and-dash boys.
Siren-fed boys.
Fatherless boys
siring boys. Noise
them. Urban
reservation—hunt
and gather boys.
Keep the blood
on the reservation.
Hunt them boys.
Solve for X: how many
*why*s and zombies
equal them boys.
Give me dap
those boys. *My boy.*
My cousin. No taller than tree
trunks chopped. Those boys
sundown colorful,
watch those boys.
Southeast hocus pocus—
you see then don't see those
boys. Then you read those
boys: police blotter those
boys. Then they're ink
those boys—RIP
graffiti on white tees:

those boys. Those Clay Terrace
boys. Those
Benning Park boys. Those
River Terrace boys. Those
Drama City boys.

INTERNAL LEGISLATION

If I had the votes, I would pass the law
against loving you. The joints and sinews of my fingers
bend in opposition to the bill, voting instead
in favor of phone calls to the florist. Voting instead
for protected status for old text messages whose habitats
are threatened by exposure to swelling light.
The nerves rail about the shutdown of serotonin
pipelines. The pelvic bone whips votes to have your weight
restored there, wants evening as evening again, meaning
soft. Whole caucuses vote "no." The eyes vote "aye"—
fed up with the aching tariff they must pay
when they import the pixels of your face.
The heart votes present, weary of the reactionary
politics of my pain, fearful all its gerrymandering cannot hold.

GLASS, ONCE SHATTERED, FLUTTERS LIKE PAPER

I have never shared my waking body with that of a woman
who claimed whiteness. And only once in a dream. We were inside
my sub-mind's rendering of a midtown flat
overlooking the common comb of thermoplastic hexes on concrete.
Up high, I hoisted Sarah Jessica Parker (recall, I said dream)
upon the kitchen island, then lifted myself into her. That is the closest
I have ever intimated myself to a "white" woman. O fright,
how rich it felt for a dream, and still how true the ache
against coming. A skintight pleasure as strong as though I was myself
and the father of myself watching myself take from world
what I, as a father, never captured. *Attaboy. Give it to her.*
And I was—my hips in a demolition trance. Harder was nothing
she needed to demand. Why Sarah Jessica Parker? I don't know,
though she predicated the city and the flat. When my lucid distrust
of it all woke me, I felt the odd weight of woman's arm
reaching over my hips—my friend's hand
pistoning over my length. How delicately it had to have started or
how deeply I must have been sleeping to dream rather than flail
the moment she'd touched the part of me I protect like it's a wound.
What it took to untangle my arms, grab her wrist, and
rather than break it, guide it gently, silently, back
over the border of my thigh. Today, I recall no debrief—I maybe said
nothing. But a thing I might now call trauma may have redacted
that night's remainder. I have only carried forward the guilt
about the dream—that maybe it wasn't a pop culture coincidence,
that within, a desire for a "white" body breathes aside the wheezing
memory of the one "white" woman my father loved. Can I tell you
that story? It was the '70s and he, a young man, brought her home—
to the house on Custer Avenue—and my grandmother, my aunt,
let a kindness hush their niggling incredulity. I don't know, but
I imagine they fed her. My father planned to meet her parents
the day she graduated from a college nearby. He drove. He walked
through the bright profusion of folding chairs and trimmed grass.

When he caught her eye, the "white" woman (I will never ask
her name), he waved but she would not see him.
He kept approaching while she just kept moving away—
receding into the Jersey summer with the people she publicly loved.

LOVE BE A SLOW-MOVING STORM

Love, come cast your body
across the city, burgeoning
and rubenesque—your gaze trained
to the west from whence you came,
where you gathered. Bared flesh in churn,
Love, give not a damn for our commutes.
Love, make from seconds sloshing cubic feet, trans-
form intersections into stalling pits. Conjure rivers
from roads. None die from drowning. We are bred and born
submerged. We stumble away from our mothers forgetting
how to huff any substance but air. Love, fill the lungs underneath
the city. Flush our toxins into the bay. Then beckon back the bay, Love,
to take our sidewalks in a surge. Bathe we in we. You know I am in no rush
to be anything but this breathing conundrum—an inorganic anomaly known
as personhood. But observe, Love—the dust of me already rising as it seeks
some heaven, hoping to atomize, flock, and perch on parched high ground.
Scalp fleck and eyelash and lip chaff and exhaust, exhaust from heart
and lungs—all wanting to become finch and egret and canary, hawk
and loon. So, Love, suppress their lifting from me. Be there
no aviaries above you. Come slowly, draping rain's chain-
mail around my body. May nothing pierce or leave
my skin. Keep my ghost subdued and, if it must be,
drunk—an evaporation risk. Love, we live
between two seas, both current-wracked and
hemmed at the offings. May you, Love,
wind-rip our world along those creased
edges, discard all of this packaging—
infrastructure wilted upon the earth.

ANOTHER WAY TO UNDERSTAND OUR FATHERS

We show up, years beyond
the animus, in the places

        that managed to keep them
        adrift or away from home—

the pubs and hash-'n'-eggs
counters in other towns

        that answered our mothers'
        where the hell is he,

before we learned and before
where worked itself into *why.*

        Maybe we show up with them,
        indulging the now leathery men.

Or maybe we are alone
and they since crumbled.

        Either way, we take a stool.
        Either our fathers introduce us

or the remnants of their faces
in our own wink to others' eyes.

        Yeah, you're _____'s kid.
        I remember you says a waitress,

a barkeep we've never met—
serving us a gratis plate

        or pour of something. And somehow
        they can recount all the trifles

of distinction in our lives—voices
filling us more than any page

        in the thin scrapbook titled *Better*
        Days bound between our temples.

ACROSS SPACE AND TIME

She is my mother
in another reality
where she had not
dozens of siblings
nor an ailing mother.
In that life, I will not be
born—when her hips
meet my father's
in force, she has not
lived a hard life;
she has not raised
bushels of baby
brothers and sisters
until diapers and cries
fall inert on her
nose and ears.
In that life, she has
not been worn
down to *why not*,
and when my father
loses himself in her—
when the germ of me
begins to curl towards
nautilus—she is uncertain
enough to say *no*,
thinking it better
to nudge down
and down to null
a love I might call a life.

SMALL TRAVELER

This is not my making any ecstatic,

                              sleep-deprived screed

affirming what is reincarnation.

                Yet for so many throbs of my heart

during the self-pitying pre-dawn hours, I have

watched you on the infant monitors

                          etched in night

vision green. You sit up like a flummoxed soul

newly returned to the Earth's cradle—

                          panning, without panic,

                          the geometry of your blue-

                          walled nursery.

Outside, the sun waits to rise so that humankind can continue ending.

I am tired but not

foolish enough to presume

            the gaze you have—one that lathes the hard dark like a lighthouse

beam—

is one ignorant of our waning world.

                         Matteroffact: *she has landed here before,*

I think. Your brain a box unboxing

old maps half true, half useless atop the freshly burned

        skin of nations. *Lay back down—*

        though you are not

animated by some trance to be dislodged from.

                         Relent—

                          that too you never do.

How chafing the bed to one who has already lived a lifetime

worth of nightmare and dreaming? You soon convince

            yourself to throw over one pajama'd leg

            and lift your body across the crib rail's ledge.

You plummet—breaching into the day's painful

boundlessness, drawn again to this

            irresistible pilgrimage of falling.

ADAMAH / AMAB

I have been laboring beneath the Banner of Man since before the first rough ream of pulp was slipped into my memory's ledger. I do wonder if I can ever know the mud of who I_0 was. When one is born under a flag (for dirt, even the sun is no flag), every second is a measure of service. A flag is always on a mission. To be blazoned above other flags. Some thus must be pole. And some the anchoring concrete. Some even the conscripted breeze. It takes a team to keep a flag high. To make a flag seem like a sun. I have been called that my entire life—son. By those no father to me. I watch them on the news. I listen to them blowhard around me. Every second these days, I am wondering how I wound up part of this team. Pretending it is a family. Cased in the flag so tight it is fair to question if it is not just my skin. If the flag's desires are not actually my own. If the cadence is a violence or if violence is the cadence. All that is sure is that, steadily, we are marching. Even when I halt, the flag is marching. Over the dirt. Incredulous that there is mud still that has not surrendered. That resists the service of hardening to the shape ordained.

SUTURE

POST-OP

There is a tube in your chest. We have been monitoring
the fluid.　　　　You must remember

　　　　　　the difference between symptom and disease. We went in
　　　　　　　　not because of the fluid, but because the cuirass

around your heart was stoking the flesh. And then the body opened
its dams for leukocytes' charge and the fluid which flows

　　with it. Please voice your soreness. Do not rush to prove your returning
　　　　strength. You will live on. Some days here, then home,

where we will need you to monitor the fluid yourself. X-rays
will not be necessary. Take a moment each day to tell yourself

　　what it is you are feeling in your chest. Be it a stab or a swell, it may be
　　　　the fluid—not trying to kill you. Trying to flood you free.

ACKNOWLEDGMENTS

Prior versions of these poems first appeared in the following venues:

Academy of American Poets Poem-a-Day: "A Man with Nothing to Lose" (as "But My Chains"); "The Erotic Is a Measure Between"

American Poetry Review: "Love Be a Slow-Moving Storm"

Buzzfeed: "Minefields"

Columbia: A Journal of Literature and Art: "Across Space and Time"

Kweli Journal: "Rhythm"; "What More Could I, a Young Man, Want"

Miami Rail: "Another Way to Understand Our Fathers"

Mississippi Review: "Ronin"

The Scores: "King for a Day"

Shenandoah: "THE BOOK OF RUTH 1.2"

Virginia Quarterly Review: "Small Traveler"

Wildness Journal: "After People Stop Asking About Me"

Winter Tangerine: "Diaspora: A Narcolepsy Hymn"

NOTES

COLLECTION EPIGRAPHS ✚ President Theodore Roosevelt quoted from a graduation speech at the Washington, DC (Sidwell) Friends School; André 3000 quoted from OutKast's "Mighty 'O"; Michel Foucault quoted from the translated interview "Friendship as a Way of Life"; Prodigy quoted from Mobb Deep's "Shook Ones, Pt. II"; Doctur Dot quoted from EarthGang's "This Side."

"KING FOR A DAY" ✚ The character of Prince Canute quoted from the Vinland Saga anime, as translated from Japanese to English.

"DIASPORA: A NARCOLEPSY HYMN" ✚ Lyrics used as refrains taken from Biggie Smalls's "Juicy" and Beyonce's "Flawless."

"WHEN I SAY I WANT TO DEFUND THE POLICE" ✚ Epigraph taken from Ta-Nehisi Coates's *Between the World and Me*.

"BOOK OF RUTH, 1.3" ✚ Lyrics excerpted from LL Cool J's "Mama Said Knock You Out."

"WHAT MORE COULD I, A YOUNG MAN, WANT" ✚ Title taken from the closing line of Li-Young Lee's poem "Eating Alone."

"TRADITIONAL MARRIAGE" ✚ Lyrics excerpted from Idles' "Model Village."

"PERFORMANCE STUDIES: GUNSLINGER" ✚ The character US Marshal Matt Dillon quoted from the introduction to the *Gunsmoke* radio show.

"UNDERTAKER" +— Lyrics excerpted from Idles' "Colossus."

"PERFORMANCE STUDIES: O.P.P." +— Title taken, in part, from Naughty by Nature's "O.P.P." Other lyrics excerpted from Big Daddy Kane on Marley Marl's "The Symphony."

"INQUIRY" +— Karrine Steffans quoted from the 2015 VladTV interview "Karrine Steffans Breaks Down How She Got 'Superhead' Nickname."

"SINCE YOU AND I WOULD TALK ABOUT MARS" +— Lyrics taken from "Lush Life" by Billy Strayhorn.